Kitten Care

A Guide to Loving and Nurturing Your Pet

Kitten
Care

A Guide to Loving and Nurturing Your Pet

Kim Dennis-Bryan

LONDON, NEW YORK, MUNICH, MELBOURNE, AND DELHI

WRITTEN BY Kim Dennis-Bryan FZS

CONSULTANTS Julius Neuman BVSc (Hons), MRCVS;
Goran Zvonar BVSc, MRCVS

ORIGINAL SERIES STYLING Lisa Lanzarini

DESIGNERS Cathy Tincknell and Nick Avery

PUBLISHING MANAGER Cynthia O'Neill Collins

ART DIRECTOR Mark Richards

DTP DESIGNER Dean Scholey

CATEGORY PUBLISHER Alex Kirkham

PRODUCTION Claire Pearson

First American Edition, 2004

Published in the United States by
DK Publishing, Inc.
375 Hudson Street
New York, New York 10014

04 05 06 07 08 10 9 8 7 6 5 4 3 2
Copyright © 2004 Dorling Kindersley Limited

The publisher would like to thank the following for their kind
permission to reproduce their photographs:

(Key: a-above; c-center; b-below; l-left; r-right; t-top)

Ardea.com: John Daniels 7bc. Bruce Coleman: Jane Burton 43cr.
Corbis: Richard Hamilton Smith 6br. DK Images: Nick Avery 26cr;
Christopher Bryan 12cr, 13t; Tracy Morgan 9c. Getty Images:
Andreas Kuehn 45bl.

All other images © Dorling Kindersley Picture Library:

Andy Crawford 16cra, 16tl, 16bl, 16br; Steve Lyne 1, 2-3, 4-5, 6bl,
7br, 8c, 12cl, 13b, 14bl, 14crb, 15, 17, 18b, 18cr, 19tl, 19b, 20bl,
20cr, 20-21, 21tr, 22tl, 22br, 23tl, 23tr, 23b, 24-25, 25tr, 25bl, 25br,
26tl, 26bl, 27br, 28tl, 28cr, 28bl, 29b, 29cl, 30bl, 30cr, 31, 32tl,
32-33, 33bc, 34tl, 34br, 36b, 37, 39c, 39cl, 41tl, 41, 42bl, 43c, 44b,
45tr, 46tl, 47br, 48.

A Cataloging-in-Publication record for this book
is available from the Library of Congress.

ISBN 0-7566-0388-9

Reproduced by Colourscan, Singapore
Printed and bound in Italy by L.E.G.O.

Discover more at
www.dk.com

NOTE TO PARENTS This book teaches children how to be caring, responsible cat owners. However, your child will need help and support from you, or a professional, in all aspects of their kitten's care. Don't let your child have a kitten unless you are certain that your family has the time and resources to take care of your pet for its entire life. When you see the sign: "!" in a circle, you should take special note.

NOTE TO CHILDREN In this book, we say *either* "he" *or* "she" when we talk about how to care for your kitten. This changes depending on whether the kitten in the picture is a boy or a girl, but the advice we give applies to kittens of both sexes.

Contents

INTRODUCTION 6

DIFFERENT CATS 8

EARLY LIFE 10

FINDING A KITTEN 12

CHOOSING A KITTEN 14

GETTING READY 16

COMING HOME 18

KITTEN SAFETY 20

FEEDING 22

MEET THE VET 24

HEALTHCARE 26

SETTLING IN 28

GROOMING 30

KITTEN TALK 32

KNOW YOUR KITTEN 34

TRAINING 36

GOING OUTSIDE 38

PLAYING 40

ILLNESS 42

GROWING UP 44

CAT BREED FACTS AND INDEX 46

ACKNOWLEDGMENTS 48

Kittens will make you laugh with their playful games.

Introduction

KITTENS, WITH THEIR FLUFFY COATS and large eyes, make very lovable pets. However, before you bring one into your home, you need to think very hard about whether you can really take care of a kitten. Your pet will need to be fed, groomed, and played with every day for his whole life. Do you and your family have time to do this?

Your kitten will become one of your friends.

Think carefully

Having a pet cat is a commitment for the whole family, for years to come. It can cost your parents a lot of money, since they will have to pay the vet bills and any other expenses, such as fees at a boarding kennel. You will all have to help care for your pet.

CAN YOU BE PATIENT?

You need patience to have a kitten. Young kittens play with anything and everything. Their games are very funny, but they can scratch things. If your kitten damages something of yours, can you keep calm and not be angry?

If you decide to get two kittens, they can keep each other company while you are out.

Do you have time?

What will happen to your pet during the day, while you are at school, and your parents are at work? If your kitten is going to be kept indoors all the time, he will need lots of your time and attention when you get home.

WHICH TYPE OF KITTEN?

• Do you want a kitten or an adult cat?

• Do you want a boy or a girl kitten? As adults, male cats are slightly larger and weigh around 9–13 lb (4–6 kg); adult female cats are about 2 lb (1 kg) lighter.

• Do you want a short-haired or a long-haired kitten?

• Do you want a purebred or a mixed-breed kitten? If you want a purebred, think carefully about which breed to get. Remember, a kitten's behavior is more important than his looks.

• Is your kitten going to be allowed outside? If the answer is yes, you must think more carefully about which type of kitten to get. Long-haired kittens need more grooming if they play outdoors. There is also a greater risk that your kitten will be hurt and need veterinary treatment. To prevent unwanted kittens, you will need to have an outdoor cat neutered before it is six months old.

Going on vacation

If your family is going on vacation, you will need to find someone to care for your cat while you are away. If you can't find anyone, you will have to pay for your cat to stay in a boarding kennel or pet resort. This can be expensive. A kitten must be fully vaccinated before he can stay in a kennel.

Always inspect a boarding kennel before you leave your cat there.

Take your pet to the kennel in a carrier.

Pet carrier

Most cat owners own mixed-breed cats.

Different cats

ALL ADULT CATS ARE about the same size, but they can look very different. Cats who look alike, with the same coat type, head and body shape, are called purebred cats. They belong to a particular breed, such as the Siamese. Mixed-breed cats can be any color, and usually have short hair. Here are some different breeds.

Which cat?

When choosing your kitten, think about the time you have, and if he will be allowed outside. You'll need to spend more time grooming a long-haired cat than a short-haired cat. Quiet, easygoing cats make better indoor cats than independent ones.

Birmans have white paws. The kittens are friendly and adaptable.

Ragdoll

Maine Coon

Long-haired cats

If you'd like a long-haired kitten, the quiet, gentle Ragdoll could be an ideal choice. The long-haired Maine Coon is more independent. It needs lots of stimulation if it is kept indoors.

Persian longhairs

It's quite easy to spot Persian cats: they have flattened faces, stocky bodies, and long, dense fur. They are quiet and suited to life indoors. Persians need lots of grooming to stop their fur from matting. Unlike most breeds of cats, which lose hair in spring and fall, Persians tend to shed hair year-round.

Silver shaded

Red

Blue-cream and white

The British Blue is a placid, friendly cat with a dense coat.

Short-haired cats

British Shorthair cats are placid and friendly with round faces and stocky bodies. Other short-haired cats, such as the Bengal, are less bulky and have a less dense coat. They are just as friendly and gentle.

Bengal cat

Although it looks like a wild cat, the Bengal cat has a sweet nature.

Oriental and Siamese cats

These slim, athletic cats are lively, loving pets, but they don't really like being left alone for long periods. They are intelligent, and need to play regularly. Some even enjoy being taken out for walks on a leash!

Red and white

Siamese

Lilac

Blue Exotic

Blue tabby Exotic

Exotic cats

These cats have very thick, short coats in a variety of colors. Their fur is so dense that it stands up away from their bodies. Exotic cats are playful, affectionate cats with round or flat faces, depending on the breed.

KEEPING WARM

Small kittens snuggle together to keep warm while their mother is away. These kittens are only four weeks old. They are just starting to explore their surroundings and enjoy playing with toys.

A mother cat spends a lot of time washing her kittens. It keeps them healthy.

Early life

FOR THE FIRST TWO WEEKS of a kitten's life, he is totally dependent on his mother. She will give him all the milk, love, and care he needs. By the age of six weeks, he will be much more independent. Most kittens go to new homes when they are seven to fourteen weeks old.

A caring mother

Kittens are blind and deaf when they are born. Their mother feeds them, and keeps them clean and warm until they are old enough to take care of themselves.

Mother cats lick newborn kittens clean and dry.

Endless patience

A mother cat takes very good care of her kittens, even when they are quite big and adventurous. She will still groom and play with them.

HOW A KITTEN GROWS FROM NEWBORN TO NINE WEEKS

Newborn

A newborn kitten sleeps a lot of the time. If he is hungry, he drinks milk from his mother.

One week old

The kitten is still blind, deaf, and helpless, but now he is able to cry when he is hungry.

Two weeks old

His eyes are open, and he is crawling around. He can't control his legs very well.

*Mother cats stay close
by their kittens while
they are very small.*

*A kitten pushes his front
paws against his mother's
body to get milk.*

*At this age, a kitten
drinks only his
mother's milk.*

Three weeks old

The kitten can walk, and has
his first teeth. He has started to
explore his surroundings.

Four weeks old

The kitten can run and play
with his brothers and sisters.
He is starting to wash himself.

Nine weeks old

The mixed-breed kitten
is old enough to travel to
his new home.

Finding a kitten

There are always plenty of kittens available, if you know where to look.

ONCE YOU KNOW THE TYPE of kitten you want, you can start to look for it. To find a purebred kitten, contact the Cat Fanciers Association for a list of breeders. Ask your vet if he knows of any kittens looking for new homes. Or call an animal shelter, which often needs to find homes for unwanted kittens.

Where to look

Check local newspapers for ads for kittens for sale. Also look at store notice boards, since some people advertise kittens there. You can also ask a local farmer if he has any kittens available.

If you find a kitten through your local paper, you probably won't have to travel very far to get it.

When to look

It is more difficult to get a kitten during the winter months. This is because most kittens are born between May and October.

A purebred kitten

To find a purebred kitten, such as a Burmese, contact the Cat Fanciers Association. They will tell you more about the breed, and give you a list of breeders in your area. Purebred kittens cost a lot more than mixed-breed kittens.

All purebred kittens of the same breed have similar features and temperaments. These are called breed traits.

A rescue kitten

Call your local humane society or rescue group and find out whether they have any kittens for adoption. If they do, arrange to visit with your parents to choose a kitten. The shelter staff may ask you about your family and home, and even ask to visit you. Don't worry about this—they are just making sure you can give the kitten a good home.

Animal shelters generally have lots of adult cats as well as kittens in need of homes. If you want an adult cat, shelters are the best places to find one.

Choosing between different kittens can be difficult— they're all so cute!

Purebred kittens of the same breed usually look quite similar.

Choosing a kitten

YOU CAN TELL A LOT about your kitten's health and personality the first time you meet. If he is going to be allowed outside, look for a confident kitten. An independent kitten that explores his surroundings will not be scared by the strange noises and smells he'll meet outdoors.

Purebred kittens

Usually, you visit a breeder to choose your kitten when he is only few weeks old. However, you won't be able to bring him home until he is about 14 weeks old and has been fully vaccinated. By this time your kitten should be trained to use a litter box.

Mixed-breed kittens may look very different from their siblings.

Mixed-breed kittens

Mixed-breed kittens usually go to their new homes at about seven to nine weeks old. Although you will be responsible for having your kitten vaccinated, you also have more time to enjoy your kitten while he is small.

A healthy kitten

Look for a lively, friendly kitten with bright eyes, clean ears, a cool nose, and pink gums. If he has a wet tail or a sore bottom, he may have a stomach upset. Black ear wax is a sign of ear mites, and a swollen tummy is a sign of tiny worms inside him. Both conditions can be treated using the correct products and are not a reason to reject a kitten that is otherwise healthy.

A healthy coat

Your kitten's coat should feel clean and well cared-for. There should be no stains on the fur, or any signs of fleas.

A lifelong friend

Look for a pet with a friendly personality. Try and see your kitten with her mother. If her mother is loving and relaxed, it's a good sign, as your kitten may grow up to be like that, too. Sit down and let your kitten climb over you. She should purr if you stroke her.

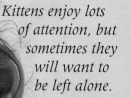

Kittens enjoy lots of attention, but sometimes they will want to be left alone.

!

A kitten shouldn't leave her mother until she is at least seven weeks old.

SIGNS OF HEALTH

1. Her eyes should be clear, bright, and without discharge.

2. The inside of her ears should be clean and pink.

3. Her gums should be pink, and the teeth white.

4. Her coat should be clean and well groomed.

5. There should be no stains on the fur around her bottom.

6. She shouldn't be coughing or wheezing.

7. She should be alert, and not too timid.

Pet stores sell lots of kitten toys, but a kitten will have just as much fun with a scrunched-up piece of paper.

Getting ready

HELP YOUR KITTEN SETTLE in to his new home by getting everything ready before he arrives. As well as buying the things you need, make sure your home is safe for your kitten to play in. Doing this early gives you more time to be with your kitten, later on.

Pet carrier

Bring your kitten home in a pet carrier. Wire or plastic cages last longest and are the easiest to keep clean. Put some newspaper in the bottom, and cover it with an old towel or a blanket, to keep your kitten warm during the trip.

Plastic-covered wire pet carrier

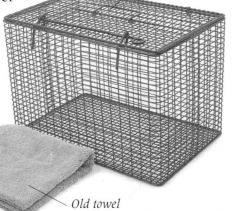

Old towel

Complete moist kitten food

Complete dry kitten food

Food and bowls

Buy separate bowls for your kitten's food and water. At first, try to feed him what he is used to eating. Complete kitten foods are popular, since nothing needs to be added. Some people prefer to feed canned kitten food or fresh foods.

Scratching post

Your kitten will sharpen his claws every day. Give him a scratching post so he doesn't scratch your furniture.

Litter box

Rubber gloves

Scoop

The litter box is where your kitten will go to the bathroom. Put it in a quiet place, away from his bed and water bowl. Try to use the litter he is used to.

Fine litter

Tray liner

Newspaper

Scratching post

Toy

Base

Warm bed

Find a quiet, draft-free spot for your kitten's bed where he can still get to his drinking water and the litter box. A cardboard box, lined with newspaper and a warm blanket, is fine to start with. Later on you can buy him a cat bed. There are many types of beds to choose from.

OTHER ESSENTIALS

- Wide-based water bowl
- Grooming tools
- Toothbrush and animal toothpaste
- Nail clippers
- Cleaning materials, such as stain remover

Items for going outside
- Cat collar and identity tag
- Cat door

Hot-water bottle

Warm blanket

Wicker basket

Give your kitten plenty of time to to settle down in her pet carrier.

Coming home

WHEN YOU GO TO PICK UP your kitten, you will probably be very excited, especially if this is the first time you have had a pet of your own. Remember not to rush your kitten. Be patient and let her do things at her own pace so she won't be frightened. Talk reassuringly to your kitten during the trip to your house so she starts to get used to the sound of your voice.

Be considerate

Remember, your kitten is leaving her home and her family, and she may be a little scared. Try to pick her up before a weekend or during a school vacation when she can settle in to your normal daily routine. Avoid holidays, birthdays, or other busy, noisy times.

Kittens usually settle down quickly.

Arriving home

When you arrive home, let your kitten come out of the carrier in her own time. Then show her where her food and water bowls are, and where you have put the litter box. Keep her in one room for a few days until she settles in.

Wait for your kitten to come to you to be petted.

As soon as you arrive home, let your kitten watch you as you fill the litter box. It is a good way of showing your kitten where it is.

Meeting other pets

Watch when your kitten meets your other pets in case they get jealous of one another and become aggressive. Given time, they will become good friends.

After a while, your pets will get used to each other and live together quite peacefully.

Meeting your friends

Your friends will want to come and see your new kitten as soon as you arrive home. You, as the proud new owner, will be equally eager to show your kitten off to them. It's difficult, but be patient, and let your kitten get used to your family and home before you invite your friends over.

Ask friends to talk quietly to your kitten so she isn't scared.

Kittens must not go outside until they have been vaccinated. Keep windows and outside doors closed.

Kitten safety

KITTENS ARE NATURALLY CURIOUS. Your kitten will examine every corner of your home when he has settled in. He will explore everything he can reach, and this might lead him into trouble. Keeping your kitten safe is very important. You need to look around the house, and the yard if he is to be allowed outside, and make sure there are no hidden dangers.

Holding your kitten

Kittens are small and flexible, so you must be careful how you pick them up. Your kitten needs to feel safe and secure, so support his weight by placing one hand under his chest and the other around his back end. Then hold him against you.

Hold your kitten gently but firmly.

Look out!

Playing with cords is dangerous. Your kitten may get a deadly shock if you leave them plugged in.

Electric wires

Kittens love to play with string, and they see wires and cords as extra-big string! Turn off appliances and pull out plugs when you aren't using them, so your kitten doesn't give himself an electric shock.

Taking care

Stop your kitten from touching houseplants. They may make him ill if he eats the leaves. Put away small objects, like buttons and needles, that your kitten might swallow and choke on. Remove tablecloths so he won't try to climb them and bring plates or vases crashing down.

Keep kittens away from spilled paint, bleach, and cleaning fluids—they can poison themselves when they lick their wet paws or clean their fur.

Place houseplants on shelves where your kitten can't reach them.

Poisons

Keep dangerous substances, such as paint and household detergents, in cupboards with child safety latches so your kitten cannot get at them. Don't let your kitten in the garage—for some reason, cats are attracted to antifreeze! There is also a danger he will slip into your parents' car, or go to sleep under it, without anyone noticing he is there.

SAFETY CHECKLIST
• Put dangerous substances in a latched cupboard.

• Keep garage doors shut.

• Keep washing machines and dryers shut.

• Put screens in front of fires.

• Put houseplants high up out of reach.

• Unplug electrical appliances.

• Beware of small objects that your cat can swallow.

• Don't let your kitten walk or sit on kitchen countertops.

Feeding

YOU ARE RESPONSIBLE for feeding your kitten at regular times every day so he will grow up strong and healthy. At first, try to give him the same kitten food he ate in his first home, because this is what he is used to. Introduce any changes to his diet over a few days so he has time to adjust. Sudden changes may give him an upset stomach.

Your kitten will quickly learn when it is mealtime. He'll come looking for food!

What to feed

Giving your kitten complete kitten foods means you can be sure he is getting a balanced diet. If your kitten refuses to eat kitten food, ask your vet for advice. Make sure your kitten always has fresh water to drink.

Water bowl

Complete moist kitten food

Grass

Even indoor kittens should have access to a little grass.

Eating grass

It may sound strange, but cats sometimes need to eat a little grass! It helps them to get rid of fur balls, which are formed from hair swallowed while cats are grooming themselves.

BEING NEAT
To keep the floor clean, place your kitten's food and water bowls on an old newspaper.

1 Kittens like to be able to smell their food, so take cans out of the refrigerator at least 30 minutes before mealtime so the food can warm up.

2 The amount you feed your kitten at each meal depends on his age and weight. Use your kitten's own spoon and fork to serve his food.

3 Kittens have tiny stomachs, so feed them frequent, small meals. Any leftover moist food should be cleaned up.

Always wash your kitten's feed bowls thoroughly after he has eaten.

HOW MANY MEALS?

Age	Meals per day
Under 3 months	4 meals
Up to 5 months	3–4 meals
5–6 months	2–3 meals
over 6 months	2 meals

Your kitten should be eager to come and eat at mealtimes.

Meet the vet

TAKE YOUR KITTEN to the vet as soon as possible after you bring him home. The vet will examine him to make sure he is healthy. She will also vaccinate him if necessary. Try to find a vet near your home so you can get there quickly in an emergency. A short trip is also easier for your kitten if he is feeling ill.

Take your kitten to the vet for a checkup even if he has been vaccinated.

First appointment

If your kitten hasn't been fully vaccinated, keep him away from other animals. Visit the vet at the end of office hours, or wait in the car until it is your turn.

At the vet's, encourage your kitten to leave his carrier but don't rush him.

Inoculations

By having your kitten vaccinated (at two, three, and four months), you protect him from several serious illnesses. A week after the last injection, your kitten can go outside, but he'll need to have a booster injection every year. Your kitten will also need an injection to protect him from rabies. Your vet will tell you when to bring your kitten for his shots.

Your kitten's shots may be listed on a special card.

Your vet will trim your cat's claws if they are too long.

Boy or girl?

It is a good idea to ask the vet to check whether your kitten is a boy or a girl. It isn't easy to tell the two apart unless you are an expert!

The female kitten is on the left and the male on the right.

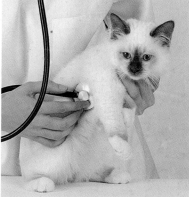

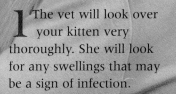

1 The vet will look over your kitten very thoroughly. She will look for any swellings that may be a sign of infection.

2 She will make sure his eyes are clear and bright and there is no discharge. She will look in his ears for black ear wax, which is a sign of ear mites.

3 She will also listen to his heart using a stethoscope. The beat should be regular, though it may be slightly faster than normal if he is nervous.

Healthcare

YOUR VET KNOWS a lot about kittens, including how to keep them healthy. She can show you exactly what you must do to care for your kitten, and explain why it is important. Some things need to be done every day, others weekly or at regular intervals. Keep a record book so you know when things need to be done.

Get your kitten used to having his teeth brushed while he is young.

Worming

Worming powder

The vet may tell you to "worm" your kitten monthly until he is six months old, and then every 12 weeks to get rid of tiny worms living in his tummy. She may give you a powder to mix into his next meal. Mix it in well—some kittens don't like taking medicines.

Small toothbrush

Animal toothpaste

Tooth care

The vet will show you how to brush your kitten's teeth. Do this every day and you will help stop tooth decay and gum disease later on.

SAFETY TIP

Cats hate taking medicines. If your kitten gets upset, wrap him in a blanket so he can't scratch you, and ask for help from an adult.

Giving medicines

It's difficult to give tablets to a kitten, even if the pills are hidden in a tasty treat. The vet will show your parents what to do. You can help by keeping your pet calm, and hugging and petting her afterward.

1 First, try to get your kitten to relax by talking to her quietly. Hold her head firmly, but gently, so she can't bite you.

2 Next, open her mouth. To do this, put your index finger and thumb behind the longest upper teeth. Use your free hand to open her jaw.

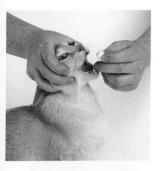

3 Place the pill in her mouth. Put it as far back on her tongue as you can. Let her close her mouth, but do not let her go yet.

4 Encourage her to swallow by stroking her throat. You must watch your kitten carefully to make sure she doesn't spit the pill out again.

CHIPPING

Ask your vet about identity chipping. A tiny chip, which can be read electronically, is injected into your kitten's neck. If your kitten gets lost, the chip tells people how to contact you.

grain-sized chip

Keeping records

Label a file with your kitten's name and keep important information in it, such as her vaccination certificate and your vet's phone number.

Make a note in your diary so you know when your cat's worming and annual injections are due.

Settling in

YOUR KITTEN WILL FEEL a little lost when you first bring her home. You can help her settle in by establishing a routine from day one. Feed her at regular times and set aside time to play with her, groom her, or simply be close by. Use her name often so she gets used to it. Keep her in one room until she gets to know it, then let her explore further.

Outdoor cats appear a few minutes before mealtimes.

Look out for trouble

Your kitten will explore more each day as her confidence increases. It is up to you to keep her safe, so be on the lookout if she starts climbing. She may get stuck, knock something over, or eat something she shouldn't. Try to discourage climbing in the house.

To stop your kitten from climbing, lift her off any high surfaces she climbs onto.

Put your kitten's litter box on newspaper to reduce mess.

Changing the litter

A cat's toilet is called a litter box. Put your kitten's litter box in a quiet corner. When he uses it, remove the soiled litter since your kitten won't go in a dirty tray. Each week, change the litter completely. Always wear rubber gloves and use a litter shovel.

BEING ALONE

Remember your kitten is used to snuggling up with her brothers and sisters to sleep. To help her settle at night, give her a warm hot-water bottle wrapped in a blanket. This, and a ticking clock, will stop her from being lonely.

You will find it easier to remember to do things if you have a set daily routine.

Playing

Make your kitten happy by playing with her. She'll enjoy playing with a toy, such as a squeaky mouse.

Kittens use their claws to grab toys. Be careful not to get scratched.

Sleeping

Your kitten will sleep a lot, often in unexpected places. Let her rest whenever she wants to. Avoid handling her too much over the first few days.

Let your kitten rest in her basket when she is tired of playing.

Kittens use their rough tongues and their paws to groom themselves.

Grooming

KITTENS SPEND LOTS OF TIME licking their coats to remove loose hairs, and using their paws to wash their faces. This is called grooming. If you have a long-haired kitten, you will need to help with his grooming every day. This will keep his coat soft, clean, and free from tangles. If your kitten gets used to being groomed while he is young, the job will be much easier when he gets older.

Why groom?

Grooming your kitten keeps his coat in good condition. It also prevents long-haired kittens from getting matted coats. By brushing away loose hairs, you stop your kitten from swallowing them when he grooms himself. You also stop his hairs from being left around the house and on the furniture.

Flea comb

Brush

Short-haired kittens need to be groomed about once a week.

Chamois

Grooming tools need to be kept clean and neat.

Checking for fleas

Your kitten will like being groomed by you, since cats often groom each other. While grooming him, check his coat for fleas by looking for black specks in his fur. If you find them, ask your vet for a suitable treatment.

1 Always start a grooming session with your kitten by petting him. When he is relaxed, start to brush him gently. Begin on his back and work toward his tail.

2 Brush his tummy next. Untangle knots in the coat at the top of his legs, since they can be uncomfortable.

3 Check his eyes. If they are crusty, or there is an overflow of tears, use a damp pet tissue to clean them.

4 When you are finished grooming, pet your kitten. If he is happy, he will purr.

31

Kitten talk

YOUR KITTEN CAN "TALK" to you in lots of ways. She'll meow to get your attention, and purr loudly when she is happy. She'll use her eyes, ears, tail, and even her claws to tell you things. If you understand what your kitten is saying, you can respond by petting her, or playing a game with her.

A kitten will soon learn to tell you what she wants.

Kittens rarely meow to other cats, but they do meow at people.

Purring

When kittens are happy, they make a soft rumbling sound, called purring. If you stroke your kitten gently as she settles on your lap, she'll probably start to purr. She's telling you that she's warm and happy. She'll half-close her eyes, and may also start to knead or "paddle" on your knees with her paws.

Meowing

Kittens meow when they are hungry, or if they want to come in or go out. Your kitten's voice will become so familiar that in time you will recognize it even if you can't see her.

Hissing

If your kitten is frightened, she will make a hissing noise. Don't try to pick her up or she may bite or scratch you. Talk to her reassuringly, but leave her alone until she feels better. When she comes to you, pet her gently.

A frightened kitten puts her ears slightly back and hisses loudly.

Even when your kitten is dozing, she can purr loudly.

BODY CONTACT

Your kitten will start to rub up against things as she settles into your home. When she does this, she is leaving her scent on the object. It's the same when she rubs up against your hand or leg. You can't smell anything because your nose is not as sensitive as hers. She is telling you she accepts you as part of her family.

Kittens put their ears forward when they are happy and back if they are scared.

Licking

A contented kitten will sometimes lick your hands. Her tongue will feel dry and rough on your skin. This is because the surface is not smooth, but covered with lots of little barbs.

Know your kitten

KITTENS HAVE MOODS, just as we do. As well as meowing, purring, or hissing, a kitten uses his whole body to express himself. You'll quickly learn to recognize when your kitten is happy, playful, frightened, or angry. If he is happy or playful, he'll probably come to you for attention. If he is scared, he'll show it. His hair will literally stand on end. If your kitten is angry, don't touch him or he may scratch you.

Your kitten is your friend, so it's important to try to understand what he is saying to you.

Being content

You can't mistake a contented kitten. He will be totally relaxed, often with his eyes half-closed. However, if he is disturbed, he will be immediately alert.

As kittens relax, they usually get sleepy, too.

Using his tail

You know your kitten is happy when he carries his tail straight up. If he is frightened, he fluffs out his tail. If he is angry, he swishes his tail from side to side. If he twitches just the tip of his tail, he is concentrating hard on something, such as a toy or a game.

Being playful

If your kitten feels playful, he may stalk a toy to practice his hunting skills. He may also ask you to play by rolling over and gently batting the air with his paws.

Kittens stalk by crawling along on their tummies.

The bristling fur of this kitten's tail shows he is scared of something.

Being scared

If your kitten is scared, he'll try to make himself look bigger. He does this by fluffing up his tail and arching his back. The black central parts of his eyes will become large and round.

Tail raised over back

Arched back

Forward-pointing ears

Stretching after a nap is different from being scared.

CLIMBING

Kittens use their claws to climb and to defend themselves. Some cat owners ask their vet to surgically remove a kitten's claws so he can't scratch their furniture. This operation hurts the cat and makes it hard for him to climb.

Stretching

When your kitten stretches, he will arch his back and raise his tail. You will know he is happy, not scared, because his hair lies flat against his body, and his eyes don't change.

Night vision

Kittens can see in the dark much better than you can. This is because they have a mirrorlike layer at the back of their eyes that reflects light. It allows them to see in the dim light at dawn and dusk, the times of day when cats are most active.

Always keep your kitten on a leash if you take her out for walks.

Training

THERE ARE LOTS OF THINGS you can teach your kitten, from litter-training to recognizing her name. When she knows her name, train her to come when you call. You can also teach her the meaning of "no." Whatever happens, be patient. Never, ever hit your kitten.

Litter training

Put your kitten's litter box in a quiet corner. Every few hours, and after she has eaten, lift your kitten into the box. She will soon learn this is where she must go to the bathroom. She may have a few accidents at first. If you catch her not using the tray, scold her so she knows she has done wrong.

Most kittens learn quickly, and start using their litter boxes when they are about three weeks old.

Always reward good behavior with praise and a treat.

Coming when you call

Your kitten must learn to come when you call her, especially if you let her go outside. First, she must learn her name, so use it often. Then, before giving her a meal, call her to you. Offer her a food treat, and sound pleased if she comes when you ask.

Traveling

If your kitten doesn't like being put in a pet carrier, she may get very angry and stressed. This is a problem if you want to take her anywhere. Get her to relax by putting food treats in the carrier when you are at home, without shutting her inside.

If you take your kitten to the vet, or on vacation, she has to travel in a pet carrier.

SCRATCHING

As soon as you bring your kitten home, give her a scratching post. Otherwise, she may claw furniture and carpets. It's harder to correct bad behavior than to stop it from occurring in the first place!

Saying "no"

Training takes time. Be patient and never lose your temper.

If your kitten ignores you when you tell him not to do something, you may need to take further action. If you are indoors, say "no" firmly, and spray him with a little water. Do it quickly so he doesn't see you. Kittens hate being wet, and they usually stop what they are doing after a couple of sprays.

You must discipline your kitten if he is being naughty.

37

Supervise your kitten if she goes outside. She may climb up somewhere and then be scared to jump down.

Going outside

WHATEVER YOUR KITTEN'S AGE, you must keep her indoors for two weeks after you bring her home so she can settle in. After that, your kitten can go outside one week after she's been vaccinated. Small kittens rarely go far, but you should still watch her whenever she goes outdoors. Make sure she is wearing her collar and identity tag when she goes out.

Using a cat door

Your kitten may not want to use a cat door at first. Hold the flap open so she can go through it without pushing against it. Use food treats to encourage her. As your kitten gets bigger and heavier, she will find it easier to push the flap aside.

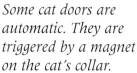

Some cat doors are automatic. They are triggered by a magnet on the cat's collar.

Intrepid climbers

Kittens get braver as they get more confident. If your kitten starts to climb trees, don't let her get beyond your reach. She is not an experienced climber and may get frightened. You need to be able to rescue her easily if she gets scared and won't climb down on her own.

Adult cats are skillful climbers, but kittens are not. They learn how to climb as they grow up.

Cat collar

ID (identity) tags

Buying a collar

Buy a special kitten collar with a stretchy section. This will extend if the collar gets caught on anything. Attach an ID tag with the kitten's name and your parent's phone number.

HUNTING

Hunting is natural for a kitten, but you may not like it if your pet brings you what she has caught. If you fix a bell to her collar, she can still hunt, but she won't catch anything. Birds and mice will hear the bell long before she gets close enough to catch them.

Make sure your kitten's collar fits properly. You should be able to slip two fingers between the collar and her neck.

Your kitten's games can be great fun to watch, especially at first, when his coordination is not very good.

Playing

YOUR KITTEN LEARNS about the world around him by playing games. He stalks, chases, and pounces on his brothers and sisters and his toys. This helps him develop his hunting skills. Playing also gives him mental and physical exercise. This is particularly important for keeping him busy if he is to spend his life totally indoors.

Learning to play

Kittens love to play and explore. During their first weeks, they spend most of their waking hours wrestling, and play-fighting with their brothers and sisters. Meanwhile, their mother keeps a watchful eye on them all and makes sure they are safe.

A simple ball makes a great toy!

Playing is fun!

Kittens will stalk and pounce on almost anything that moves, so they can easily be tempted to play. You can make your own toys for your kitten, using a scrunched-up scrap of paper and string. Alternatively, you can buy a ping-pong ball, or lots of different kinds of cat toys, from your local pet store.

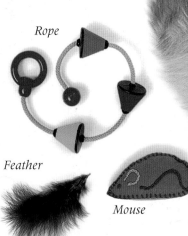

Rope

Feather

Mouse

SLEEPY KITTEN

The time you spend playing with your kitten will help to keep him healthy, bright, and fit. Remember, though, that kittens get tired quickly. So if your kitten wants to sleep instead of playing, you must let him rest.

(!) Kittens may try to scratch you when they are tired of playing.

You can easily make a kitten toy by tying a piece of paper to a ribbon.

If your kitten vomits more than once, consult your vet.

Illness

WHEN ANIMALS ARE SMALL, they can get sick very quickly, and kittens are no exception. Luckily, they bounce back just as fast and then want to make up for lost time! If this is your first kitten, be extra-careful when you're looking for signs of illness. In time, you will know when your pet is feeling ill. Take your kitten to the vet immediately if you think there is a serious problem.

FLEAS

If your kitten is scratching more than usual, check its fur for fleas. If you find them, ask your vet for advice. You shouldn't use a flea collar, or insecticides, on a kitten under 12 weeks old.

Cat flea

• *Actual size of cat flea*

Minor injuries

If your kitten has a minor cut or graze, clean the wound carefully and check it is not serious. Then treat it with an antiseptic wash. (Use one that won't upset your kitten's tummy if he licks the wound). Any swelling or redness should disappear in a few days. However, if you are at all worried, ask your vet for advice.

Gently clean any cuts and grazes to see how serious they are. Deep cuts need to be seen by a vet.

Emergencies

If your kitten is in pain, or bleeding from an injury, take him to the vet right away. Kittens easily go into shock. Pain may make your kitten crabby, so take extra care when you move him. Put him in a cage, or a box lined with a blanket, so he doesn't move around too much.

If your kitten is ill, wrap him in a blanket and comfort him.

Sick kitten

Warm blanket

THE THIRD EYELID

Like people, kitten's eyes have an upper and a lower eyelid. However, kittens also have a third eyelid, which helps to protect their eyes. Usually, you cannot see this eyelid, but if a kitten is ill, the third eyelid may appear in the inner corners of the eyes.

**Watch out:
A sick kitten
may try to
scratch you.**

Growing up

KITTENS GROW UP QUICKLY. They are full-grown at about six months. Even when she is an adult cat, your pet will rely on you for food and shelter every day of her life. You are responsible for her general happiness, too, and so you will have to make certain decisions.

Most cats live well into their teens. Elderly cats sleep a lot and may need special care.

Kittens enjoy playing, but they also enjoy hugs and attention.

Neutering

To prevent a female cat from having babies, have her neutered. This is an operation the vet can perform. Male cats who are neutered have fewer fights, and all neutered cats are less likely to run away from home.

If you let your cat have kittens, you will have to find homes for them all.

Getting older

As your cat gets older, she may start to act a little differently. An older cat often sleeps more and plays less. She may also pay less attention to her coat. If this happens, you will need to groom her more often. Older cats get sick more easily, too. You can ask your vet for advice about how to keep her healthy.

As your cat gets older, she will need regular veterinary checkups to keep her happy and healthy.

MOVING

Moving can upset a cat. Keep your cat inside for about two weeks, until she has settled in. Keep her in one room at first. Then let her start to explore. Rub a cloth over her fur and dust the doors with it. Smelling her scent around the new home will make her feel more secure.

Overweight cats do not live as long as slim, fit ones.

Fat cats

When your cat grows up, she will eat adult cat food, not kitten food. Change her diet slowly. Don't give her too much food—fat cats are not as healthy as slim cats. As she grows older, you may need to change her diet again. Ask your vet for advice about this.

A sweet nature is more important than good looks.

Cat breed facts

THE TABLE BELOW shows the coat type of some of the more popular cat breeds. It also gives an idea of the most noticeable personality traits. Look for more information about cats on the web (see recommended web sites, below).

BREED	COAT TYPE	TEMPERAMENT
Persian Longhair		
Ragdoll		
Birman		
Norwegian Forest		
Angora		
Tiffany		
Turkish Angora		
Turkish Van		
Balinese		
Maine Coon		
Somali		
Siamese		
Bengal		
British Shorthair		
Tonkinese		
Chartreux		
Exotic Shorthair		
Burmese		
Oriental Shorthair		
Korat		
Cornish Rex		
Abyssinian		
American Shorthair		
European Shorthair		
Mixed-Breed Cat		Any combination of the above

Recommended web sites
www.fanciers.com
www.cfinc.org

KEY

COAT TYPE

long hair	short hair

TEMPERAMENT

People-oriented	Independent
Intelligent	Inquisitive
Gentle	Active/Energetic

Long-haired kitten

Short-haired kitten

Index

A
Abyssinian 46
adult cat 7, 13
American Shorthair 46

B
Balinese 46
Bengal 9, 46
Birman 8, 14, 46
boarding 6
British Blue 9
British Shorthair 9, 46
brushing teeth 26
Burmese 12, 46

C
cables and wires 20
cat bed 17
cat collar 17, 38, 39
cat door 17, 38
Chartreux 46
claws 25, 29, 32, 35
climbing 28, 35, 38
collar 17, 38, 39,
Cornish Rex 46

E
early life 10, 11
emergencies 45
European Shorthair 46
exotic cat 9
Exotic Shorthair 46

F
feeding 22, 23
fleas 14, 30, 42
food 11, 16, 22, 23, 26
food bowls 16, 18, 23
fur balls 22

G
grass 22
grooming 7, 30, 31
grooming tools 17, 30
growing up 44, 45

H
health 14, 15, 25
healthcare 26, 27
hissing 33, 34
holding a kitten 20
housebreaking *see* litter
training
hunting 39

I
identity chips 27
identity tag 17, 39
illness 21, 42,43
independent cat 8, 14
indoor cats 8

L
licking 33
litter box 14, 16, 18,
19,28, 36
litter training 36
long hair 7, 8, 30, 46

M
Maine Coon 8, 46
medicines 26, 27
meeting friends 18
meeting other pets 18
meowing 32, 34
mixed-breed kitten 7, 8,
11, 12, 14, 46
mites 14, 25
moving 45

N
nail clippers 17
neutering 44
night vision 35
Norwegian Forest 46

O
Oriental cat 9
Oriental Shorthair 46
outdoor cats 28
overweight cats 45

P
pedigree *see* purebred
Persian Longhair 9, 46
pet carrier 16, 18, 24, 37
plants 21
playing 29, 40,41
purring 15, 31, 32,33, 34
poisons 21
purebred kitten 7, 8,
12, 14

R
Ragdoll 8, 46
record book 26, 27

S
safety 20, 21
scent marking 33
scratching 6, 16, 35,
37, 42
scratching post 16, 37
short hair 7, 8, 9, 30, 46
Siamese 8, 9, 46
sleep 10, 29, 41, 44, 45
Somali 46

T
tail 31, 34,35
third eyelid 43
Tiffany 46
Tonkinese 46
toothbrush 17, 26
toothpaste 26
toys 16, 40,41
training 36,37
traveling 37
Turkish Angora 46
Turkish Van 46

V
vacations 7
vaccination 7, 14, 20,
24, 25, 38
vet 24, 25, 26, 27, 42,
44

W
water 17
water bowl 17, 18
wires *see* cables and
wires
worming 26

ACKNOWLEDGMENTS

DORLING KINDERSLEY WOULD LIKE TO THANK:
The Mayhew Animal Home and Humane Education Centre for the
black, and black-and-white mixed-breed kittens;
Helen for Murray, the Birman kitten;
Betty for Smartie and Geoffrey, the tortoiseshell and ginger kittens.

MODELS
Olivia, Hope, Xabi, Stefan, Gabriella, and Natalie